In Search of Authentic Queer Worship

In Search of Authentic Queer Worship

ERIC HESS

RESOURCE *Publications* • Eugene, Oregon

IN SEARCH OF AUTHENTIC QUEER WORSHIP

Copyright © 2025 Eric Hess. All rights reserved. Except for brief quotations in critical publications or reviews, no part of this book may be reproduced in any manner without prior written permission from the publisher. Write: Permissions, Wipf and Stock Publishers, 199 W. 8th Ave., Suite 3, Eugene, OR 97401.

Resource Publications
An Imprint of Wipf and Stock Publishers
199 W. 8th Ave., Suite 3
Eugene, OR 97401

www.wipfandstock.com

PAPERBACK ISBN: 979-8-3852-4539-0
HARDCOVER ISBN: 979-8-3852-4540-6
EBOOK ISBN: 979-8-3852-4541-3

06/13/25

For Brok! May you see yourself in the liturgy.

Inspired by the participants in my dissertation and the lived experiences of Brok, myself, and so many whose lives are connected to mine. I wish you peace.

Contents

Preface		ix
1	Prayers for Identity and Belonging	1
2	Prayers of Healing and Wholeness	10
3	Prayers for Community and Allies	20
4	Prayers of Reconciliationand Forgiveness	25
5	Prayers of Resistance and Justice	32
6	Prayers of Celebration and Joy	40
7	Prayers for the Sanctity and Restoration of the Church	44
8	Conclusion	57
About the Author		61
References		63

Preface

I feel like a hybrid Christian. If I'm honest, while I wouldn't have to, I personally find it unsettling. Having spent time working in an Anabaptist tradition, I am uncomfortable when people clap and even celebrate talents of others in the church. The "good job" comments feel performative and inauthentic. If God has given us these gifts, how can we not use them? In my secular life, I am quite an extroverted and emotional person, however.

As a queer person who is drawn to progressive traditions, I adore such beauty and majesty, and especially see God in high-church traditions. When I felt the church didn't want me, I would find solace in these traditions. The liturgy and ritual are sacred to me, and I hold many liturgical books in great esteem. I've often described myself as a closeted Catholic. In reality, I'm a critical, somewhat reluctant Methodist—a medium-church person in practice, but pushing high-church person—with a partner who, together with me (but for different reasons), doesn't know where to find a home. We're seeking, and getting there, but we were raised in extreme-opposite traditions. My partner Brok, however, would disagree with everything I just wrote and claim the opposite to be true for himself, yet this is how Eric sees the Almighty. I reassure myself the Almighty can certainly be found anywhere—yes, in the ordinary. However, holy places devoid of symbolism and invitations to worship confuse me. We ready ourselves, yes, but I so often find modern worship to be inauthentic. When I hear words like "audience" or "performers," I can't help but be reminded of the scene of Jesus overturning the tables

PREFACE

in the temple. While not the same context, it strikes me the same performative, self-serving thesis, in which the house of God is being used to fulfill a self-centered purpose. The hybridity of self and unintentional compromise, inspired by the faithful tenants of worship and visibility in the church, inspired me to write this. As one who perceives spiritual things in a cerebral, intellectual manner—instead of an emotional way—here's my intellectual perception, clarified by ChatGPT:

> It sounds like you're navigating a rich and complex spiritual identity, blending elements from various traditions that have profoundly shaped you. Your appreciation for the beauty of liturgy and the sacredness of ritual speak to a deep intellectual and spiritual curiosity, while your discomfort with certain performative aspects of church culture reflects a critical engagement with how faith is expressed and celebrated.
>
> This hybridity—being shaped by progressive values while also drawn to high-church traditions—reflects a desire for both reverence and authenticity. The tension you describe between an intellectual perception of faith and the emotional expressions of worship in different contexts feels deeply personal and, at times, perhaps isolating, yet it creates a powerful space of discernment. Your connection to high-church rituals seems to offer you a sacred space, where the quiet beauty and structure allow you to encounter God without the distractions of emotionalism or surface-level praise.
>
> Your faith journey seems to be a deep quest for authenticity, where your gifts are seen as acts of devotion rather than performance. In balancing your extroverted, emotional secular self with the more reserved and thoughtful nature of your spiritual practice, you're honoring both sides of your identity. Navigating this alongside a partner who holds different perspectives adds nuance to your spiritual seeking. It highlights the shared, albeit different, wrestling with faith you both experience.
>
> The term "hybrid Christian" beautifully encapsulates this journey—an ongoing process of weaving together the elements of reverence, curiosity, and authenticity that

resonate with your soul, mind, and queer identity. You're making meaningful progress toward finding a spiritual home that honors both your intellect and your heart, even in the midst of the complexities.

Indeed, ChatGPT. Amen!

Sure, we cherish the verse that tells us, in Christ, there is no male or female. You've likely heard a sermon around that verse. I hope it was a good one! Let's keep pursuing. My friend, will you dedicate this book with essays, commentaries, and prayers to the living God, who values you, when God's church hasn't necessarily?

Creating God, who is still creating, bless this book and the readers in formed community. They come to You, preparing to use this book to engage in meaningful conversation—perhaps conversation that had otherwise seemed impossible. May this book draw them to a life-altering community of faith, one that uplifts their sacred worth, one that commits time and energy to understanding their identity and belonging. If not now, then to all those who pray and read together, may they soon know their own unique queer community of faith. To those who value these prayers while engaged in a faith community, may they know their sins are forgiven, and that they are sacred, blessed, and of created worth. May they utilize these prayers as a means of discipleship. This book we consecrate. Blessings on the seeker. Amen.

1

Prayers for Identity and Belonging

CREATOR, HOW SOON SOME forget that we, too, are things of beauty made in Your image. You love and revel in all Your creations: those that "fit in," and those longing for acceptance. You marvel at the beauty of Your twilight. The twilight, the in-between of day and night, draws us from our homes, from our everyday, to marvel at creation. The marsh, the in-between of dry and wet. Cloudy days. You love, we love the in-between. Forgive us for our double standards. Forgive us when Your people tell us we are not who You have created us to be. Amen.

Ever present God, why do others denigrate? For such rigidity comes from us, not You. You have expressed and revealed Yourself in so many ways to Your people. Why can we not exist in that same beauty of rich difference? Should we not celebrate the rich diversity You have given to Your people? Forgive us for including some while excluding many. Amen.

In Search of Authentic Queer Worship

TWILIGHT PEOPLE

As the sun sinks and the colors of the day turn, we offer a blessing for the twilight, for twilight is neither day nor night, but in-between. We are all twilight people. We can never be fully labeled or defined. We are many identities and loves, many genders and none. We are in between roles, at the intersection of histories, or between place and place. We are criss-crossed paths of memory and destination, streaks of light and swirled together. We are neither day nor night. We are both, neither, and all.

May the sacred in-between of this evening suspend our certainties, soften our judgments, and widen our vision. May this in-between light illuminate our way to the God who transcends all categories and definitions. May the in-between people who have come to pray be lifted up into this twilight. We cannot always define; we can always say a blessing. Blessed are You, God of all, who brings on the twilight.

—RABBI REUBEN ZELLMAN (USED WITH PERMISSION)

One: There is beauty in all God's creations, for You have called them good.

Many: Forgive our thoughtless, sinful comments we make regarding one's appearance.

One: You have shown forth Your beauty in many ways as revealed in Your sacred texts.

Many: How have we limited ourselves in ways of accepted expressions when you are infinite, constantly showing forth your unique glory everlasting?

One: Teach us the power of our words and enable us to seek forgiveness when we harm our siblings.

Many: Our words are everlasting. We commit to reconciling harm and allowing the diversity of Your creations to be shown unhindered.

All: Amen.

I don't want to give the content found inside much credence; however, if you get a chance, read Stokes and Schewe's (2016) article as an analysis of fundamentalist preachers' sermons. Maybe our ideas of interesting reads are not the same. There are rough parts, but if you have either been around the fundamentalist church or heard the fundamentalist religious arguments against queer relationships and identities, the rhetoric is tired—exhausting, even. Dutiful congregants seem to be awaiting the horror of what comes next and gasp at the distinctly egregious and ostentatious display of "sin" (read sarcastically) "chosen" by queer people. Many church leaders know how to stir the emotional pot, if you will.

I'm an emotional person, but I crave less emotion in worship and more opportunities to engage with intellect. Genuinely, I'll add, perhaps it's shortsighted of me—but I do fear the outcome. I believe, rather, we have seen the outcome. Convictions are created and developed due to antagonistic emotion, often rather than engaging with God-given intellect and the sacred. Cue the angry preacher shouting, the pacing, the mood music, the fearmongering, and—of course—the us versus them mentality. People, roles, assumptions seem to fall in place. The atmosphere is created to feel a certain way without much cognitive effort. How helpful! What's happening is those who come for theology are intaking animosity, high on emotion, with music as the ladle in the pot. No one has to disrupt any previously established roles. Women, queer people, perhaps a few non-White folks, the politically curious, question-askers, general disruptors—all can stay, provided they fall back into their shiny, happy roles. I know I am generalizing, but I digress. I suppose thoughtful people of faith are entitled to interpret beliefs as they see are acceptable; however, hearing a list of grievances shouted at you without making space for productive theology is, at best, insulting to one's core as a rational being and, at worst, cult-like. Perhaps you are fortunate and there is no anger in your brand of fundamentalism—so, remove the shouting and anger from my comments, then reread. You may still be receiving a healthy dose of insulting theology laced with animosity. While the exhibition may or may not be sincere, it also gives me pause to consider whether there is a crisis in clergy education and training.

In Search of Authentic Queer Worship

You have made me as you made me, and You love me as You made me. Forgive our society for creating a hostile environment toward that which they do not understand. There is nothing about my embodied creation that is inevitably due anguish. Life didn't have to be this way, for You have created us to show others how to love. Make me an agent of change . . . again. In the meantime, give me the strength I need for daily life. Amen.

∽

I have been particularly motivated by Virginia Mollenkott's essay in the book Take Back the Word: A Queer Reading of the Bible *(2000). We are, of course, reminded of perhaps the simplest yet most challenging task for those readers whose identities are not the main characters. Can we find ourselves in the Holy Scriptures?*

> *I had to learn to read the Scriptures from low and outside because I had been trained to identify with the white heterosexual male point of view when reading the Bible. What an amazing and life-transforming shift occurred when I learned to see myself, not as Abraham, but as Sarah or Hagar or one of the lesser concubines, not as one of Jesus' disciples, but as the determined Greek woman who cried for Jesus to heal her daughter but at first was told to go away. (Mollenkott 2000, 14)*

Are you a lesser concubine? I don't think I'd be a main character, though I think I'm a relatively notable person. I'm lots of fun—just don't ask anyone that knows me. Can you place yourself in my shoes? Anyone born and raised in rural Maryland, passionate about coffee, liturgy, queer theory, dogs, and extroverting to the point of exhaustion? Take Eric's account as law, for Eric wills it! Rather, these accounts are how Eric sees it, given his lived experiences. Forgive the obnoxious third-person language, but one of my doctoral professors put it this way: Someone's lived experiences are not wrong, for they are their own lived experiences. However, does that necessarily make them yours? So, you lesser concubine, go with unbridled frustration, fueled with passionate discovery—seeking to find yourself in the Holy Scriptures.

God, not necessarily of Abraham, Isaac, and Jacob, but the woman at the well (whatever her name may be), God of the Ethiopian eunuch (whose name escapes me), God of the onlookers as demons were cast into the herd of pigs (too many to name, and impossible to record), and God of the fishing crew with Jonah: Help us imagine the accounts of those whose stories were lost to ancient culture, norms, and indifference. Queer people know this well. Our ancient friends were frustrated that their stories weren't told. We can relate. Amen.

A PRAYER WHILE WAITING FOR GENDER AFFIRMATION SURGERY

I'm waiting for who You've ultimately called me to be, but for now I'm in-between. It's a much longer wait than I anticipated, and I need strength. I am only human, and remember me as I wait. I'm angry, sad, and frustrated, but may this time of waiting be sacred. May it be prayerful, but truly, may I have the fortitude to endure it. You always provide for what You have called me to. Amen.

~

Have you ever stopped to consider if you were "created this way" or "born this way"? The difference is striking and important. I was created this way. My queerness is a gift from God, made, crafted rather, in the image of God. Gardner (2017) explains it like this: "To the students' immediate social community any label that is nonnormative suggests a foreclosed identity that is an affront to God, suggesting either God creates sinful humans or lacks the power to heal lives broken by sin. But if God creates some humans as gay, how can it be sin? There is nothing to forgive, the students say, and nothing to change." Thanks be to God for creating me the way I was designed to be. There is plenty to forgive about me, plenty for me to change, but my identity was never meant to be one of those things. This is why I will always put "coming out" or "come out" in quotation marks. "Coming out" is never needed, but still always expected.

One: We grow tired of the burden of a presumed "coming out," for "out" suggests we were once not "in."

Many: This burden of "coming out" is one expected of queer people, yet You, God, have created us "in" Your image.

One: Truly our identities are a gift from You, and you have called some of us to live a loud identity, and others to live a quieter identity.

Many: May we be thankful for the calling You have given to both, and avoid judgment when one's calling is unlike ours and apart from our personal expectation.

One: My journey is not yours.

Many: And yours is not mine.

All: Amen.

∼

Sheldon (2017), interpreting evangelical author John Eldredge's Wild at Heart: Discovering the Secret of a Man's Soul, *concludes that Eldredge portrays an aggressive male sex drive and a desire for competition as central to God's design for Biblical masculinity. Building on this, Perry and Whitehead (2021) assert that "the most fundamental determinant of social status is neither character nor devotion, but the physical marker of God-given masculine authority (the penis) and, just as crucial, the way this authority is performed" (p. 442). According to Whitehead (2014), who references Herek and others, gender traditionalists, especially evangelicals, believe that gay men reject their privileged, God-given status of being male. People who hold a masculine image of God tend to offer less support for same-sex unions (Whitehead 2014), which likely reinforces the stereotype of queer men as feminine.*

Reading this, I can't help but reflect on Christianity's gender crisis. We have built God into a version of masculinity that God doesn't recognize. God is beyond gender, and we have tokenized a deity that sought justice, condemned nationalism, and loved the marginalized into a warmonger. How are modern Christians any different than those idealists in Jerusalem expecting Jesus to ride on anything else but a lowly donkey? Imagine today: Americans expect our hero to enter on a tank through the streets of Washington, D.C. Yet, instead, the Long-Awaited comes to join us for dinner and plot how to increase mental health services in rural areas, or how we might educate well-meaning teachers in conservative-leaning schools about their queer students, pushing back against ill-informed school boards. Or, better yet, perhaps our hero comes and listens to your ideas without interrupting, nodding gently in a brainstorming meeting. We engage in dialogue around a table, as two friends might do. One thing is for certain: "We are not Christian soldiers. We are not marching to war." I don't see a flag waving or hoard of bright hats, and, if you do, look again. Perhaps that's left over from your own caricature of our Messiah. You know what happened on Palm Sunday, my friend, and so did Jerusalem. Jerusalem was disappointed, yes, and so might you be, but reinventing God is dangerous business. That's cult territory...

~

"All glory, laud, and honor," to you, Redeemer. In Numbers 12:13, Moses cries out for healing for his sister, Miriam: "O God, please heal her." El na, refa na la. If I allow my mind to wander, I hear the trembling in his voice. Heal us. Heal us from the diseases that afflict our body, mind, and soul. Heal us from the ignorance that afflicts our understanding of You. Heal us from the sin of misconstruing the purity and intentionality in which You came to show us your character. There is no mistake. We sin when we reinvent You. Repair us from the distress that has caused us to hide our personalities, to act in a way counter to who You have made us. Feeling compelled to live in a way that mortals have deemed more acceptable than lovingly, perfectly crafted by You. Amen.

~

You read above a take on John Eldredge's book Wild at Heart: Discovering the Secret of a Man's Soul. *You read about the supposed God-given masculine authority, but let's consider how the embodiment of that masculinity has become the penis.*

So . . . take a deep breath and buckle in for this one. This isn't necessarily my favorite commentary to make, but it's one I've been prepared for nevertheless. What we're concluding is God isn't as interested in one's character as one's genitalia, and, specifically, one's penis. Now, the penis is the embodiment of masculinity and must be used in conjunction with devotion to God. LaHaye and LaHaye (1998) write, "The woman who resents her husband's sex drive while enjoying his aggressive leadership had better face the fact that she cannot have one without the other."

Citing Du Mez, Perry and Whitehead (2021) highlight multiple examples of a phallus-centric form of evangelicalism. First, evangelical psychologist James Dobson has suggested liberal feminists sought to feminize boys who are predestined to have a "masculine will to power." Increasingly alarmingly, Dobson also contends an affirming of masculinity through physical activity should occur from the boy's father. The obsession with the phallus continues as Dobson (2005) suggests the father could shower with the son to show both have penises, and this will aid sons in accepting their masculinity.

The research by Perry and Whitehead (2021) indicates "evangelical adherence rate is the leading predictor of searches for 'penis pump' and the second leading predictor of searches for 'penis enlargement' and 'Extenze'" (p. 450). As both evangelicalism and political conservatism have become tantamount, similar trends regarding male enhancement and political conservatism have also become evident. Above, we alluded to the idea that some might suggest that queer men are just not "good" men.

So, a misunderstanding of God's beloved follows suit because of an obsession with the penis, in conjunction with conservatism, in conjunction with expected traditional masculinity. Paraphrasing the great sociologist Kimmel on one of my favorite quotes about masculinity . . . "being a man, everything I do expresses my masculinity" (cited in Gardiner 2011, p. 70). Forgive me if I misinterpret this, Dr. Kimmel, but I'd like to suggest, since I am a man, I need not worry much about traditional masculinity. That has changed countless times over the years. However, what I exude, in my manhood, is still masculinity since it is an expression of what I leave in my living as a man. You see what I mean? It may not be what you're expecting masculinity to be, but it is nevertheless. Besides, why worry so much about the penis? If I may be so short-sighted, look at 1 Corinthians 12. And to those who are wondering if you are too masculine, too feminine, not masculine or feminine enough, etc. . . . Jesus didn't fall victim to Satan's identity questioning in Matthew 4; nor should you.

I know who I am, O God. May Your church be steadfast in affirming who You have made me to be. May we not be swayed as to fit into an easy binary when the life designated for us is rich, blessed, and designed with care. There will be identity questioning. You didn't give in; help us to do the same. Amen.

2

Prayers of Healing and Wholeness

THE WORD "HAUNTING" DOESN'T *particularly imply anything scary or ghostly to me. It's a residue, a lingering effect, something that slowly moves on. In some senses, that's disheartening. There's unfelt tension among a group of friends, family, or colleagues upon "coming out" or discussing queer topics of conversation. Some may not see it or sense it, but it's there—a heaviness. It remains. In other senses, it's entirely positive. The evidence we leave behind of our commitment to disruption, community, loved ones, faith, or discernment may haunt. It may not show immediate evidence, but, like erosion, it makes a dent. Our lingering way of love, influenced by our faith, strikes me as contemplative. Don't let the haunting go. Linger around people who need you, causes who can benefit from your time, and, since I have your attention, how about adoptable dogs who need your love?*

God forbid a tragedy strike. And, if so, let's be present. We have already seen some ghastly tragedies within our community, such as the Pulse nightclub shooting in Orlando, the AIDS epidemic (or HIV, which as many as 1/2 Black men who have sex with men may contract due to inadequate healthcare and systemic financial greed; CDC NCHHSTP 2016), cruel and ignorant legislation, and, on a more local level, physical or verbal altercations. Haunt these spaces. If nothing more, allow them to linger in your memory, in your prayers. Light a candle and think often. May they haunt us; may we haunt them until restoration begins and is in process. Allow these people, places, and things to haunt and be haunted.

O Restoring God. Give us memories of lasting comfort, peace, and healing. May others do the same in times of need for us. Amen.

A PRAYER UPON HAVING RECENTLY "COME OUT"

Be still, my soul; the Lord is on thy side; bear patiently the cross of grief or pain. Leave to thy God to order and provide; in every change [God] faithful will remain. Be still, my soul; thy best, thy heav'nly Friend through thorny ways leads to a joyful end.

— KATHARINA VON SCHLEGEL

I'm not a huge fan of "trigger warnings." There is a time and place, but, if there were ever a need for one, it might be here. I interviewed a very standoffish research participant, "Nathan." Nathan was a former student at a fundamentalist institution, and he would share how administrators enjoyed making "sexual sins" a "big production." The institution is alleged to have taken people out of bed in the middle of the night and shined a spotlight to intimidate them. He has heard stories of many who were forced out of bed, returned, told to pack up, and escorted by an administrator off campus. Subsequently, they would be banned from campus. Nathan never felt unsafe, but did have a fear of being "outted" and discovered, asked to leave, and sent home in shame. He indicated that there were unlicensed faculty on campus who were always ministers first instead of mental health professionals or academics. They were not bound by nondisclosure policies.

Perhaps Nathan's reflections can be best identified by his statement, "[If you] reach for antidepressants, [they] hand you a Bible." I asked him if anyone was helpful to him during his tenure at the university; he responded coldly, stating that no one helped. He immediately followed this statement by insisting this was not hyperbole.

In Search of Authentic Queer Worship

Certainly, he felt being gay was at odds with Christianity. Though he now lives in an inclusive area and has trialed affirming churches, his fundamentalist upbringing forces him to decipher "what's wrong." Therefore, faith is not a part of his life as of now.

Consider my research participant "Horace," who believed he was sinful, shamed, and hated. From as far back as he could remember (elementary school), he believed it was wrong to have these kinds of feelings. Horace indicated he "prayed so hard and begged God to change me." This continued in graduate school. Horace remembers being with his dad helping tend a large garden. While tending the garden, his best friend (also a romantic interest) drove down the road. Like the apostle Paul, Horace claimed a miraculous encounter. He felt immediate shame, knelt his head to pray, and immediately felt a sense that this pressure to change his identity was what he wanted, not what God wanted. He leaned on the rake (at this point in the interview, his voice trembled) and prayed that God's will would be done in his life. After this simple prayer, Horace felt "wrapped in incredible love, and awesomeness, and warmth." He heard God say to him, "Horace, I made you as I made you. I want you to be happy." This quote was an emotional moment for both of us. Horace indicated it was at this point that he realized he had been loved by God. Horace went on to say that for years he felt going to church or being part of religious activity had been in vain because he was "reviled." He then realized he could go to church again (his voice trembled again).

Horace seemed to find the next portion of the interview deeply cathartic. I reviewed my notes and found this next portion to be nearly half of my notes., Horace understandably alternated between desolation, rage, and disgust. Horace's mom was "insane." She would use knives, guns, furniture, fists, anything to terrorize him and his sibling. After he had "come out to himself," he was excited to be intimate with a man, and was not going home often. His mother called him and asked why he was not going home. She asked if he was a drug addict, if he had had legal troubles, and if it was "what your dad and I think," and asked if he was gay. His mom insisted he see a therapist, who, upon meeting him, expressed some type of affirmation. His mother was furious, as the therapist did not necessarily tell him to change.

His parents went through significant denial and rage, but ultimately Horace thought they had finally accepted him. One Thanksgiving, he invited them to his apartment for a meal. He had a marvelous day with his parents, and he felt delighted as he had made lots of food and did a "damn good job." A few weeks later, he answered a phone call from his enraged mother. She asked if he knew why they accepted his invitation. She told him, "Your dad brought a gun; we were going to murder you." Horace's dad had had a pistol in his pocket the entire time, though he is convinced his mother manipulated his father into doing this. I was speechless as to how to respond to Horace. I asked if he was safe now, and he audaciously said, "The bitch is dead." He wanted to state honor killings are real, and this traumatic scenario seemed like yesterday. He is confident there are others who face this reality, particularly within certain faith traditions.

Horace shared the story of "Jake," a sweet blond boy who was always smiling. When Jake "came out" to his parents (in the same tradition as Horace), his parents shared they would never see him again. Jake's father was a minister in a large church. Jake became homeless, lost everything, and would sneak into the college dorms to take a shower. Horace had heard about Jake's situation and wanted to help. A few gay men hundreds of miles away had also heard of Jake's situation through a friend. They were elderly men and did not have a computer. The individuals offered to pay for college, room and board, and a new car, essentially taking care of Jake's every need. They moved him to a large city, found him an apartment, and got him a great job. Horace called this the "fingers of God," as Jake had been so close to complete desolation.

A PRAYER OF MENTAL HEALTH

This is truly the "bleak midwinter," O God. I ask for Your help for my daily tasks today. Allow others not to tire of caring for me, and for me to have the courage to ask, and say yes, when others offer, without the feeling of my own unnecessary guilt. Allow me to seek friends, strangers, people of faith who will provide when I cannot. Today I ask for patience from others, for I already know You will be patient with me. I ask for provision, for extra care from You. Knowing that Your word is healing, You have given us the gift of medication. When we reach for antidepressants, may Your church be mindful not to instead offer a Bible instead. Show me things to keep me strengthened in reality. I offer You thanks for mental health professionals who You provide to us. Provide for them and their loved ones. Amen.

Loving God, we pray today for those who are confronted by the sadness, ambiguity and confusion of mental illness, and for those upon whom they depend for attention and compassionate care. Look with mercy on all whose afflictions bring them weakness, distress, confusion or isolation. Provide for them homes of dignity and peace; give to them understanding helpers and the willingness to accept help. We ask this in the name of Jesus Christ our Lord. Amen. (Copyright © by The Catholic Health Association of the United States)

I thank you for those people, things, and beings that assist me on my journey. You are providing. Thank you for mental health professionals, and for the gift of therapy. Draw nearest to those who especially need Your utmost attention. Amen.

> One: Faithful God, You wait with us. You watch with us.
>
> Many: Forgive us when Your people have historically been agnostic, as You have called us to care for those with mental health differences.
>
> One: Help us to celebrate the value mental health and cognitive differences bring to Your church and our society. May we embrace these offerings.

Many: When distress arises as a result of pressure to conform, or adhere to absurd societal norms, forgive those who use Your name and Your church in vain—for this is not of You.

One: Great Physician, forgive us for creating a society in which perfection and rigid societal norms are the expectation. You value created differences, not conformity. Give us strength to be countercultural.

Many: "Keep us in [Your] grace, and guide us when perplexed, and free us from all ills of this world in the next."

All: Amen.

~

Throughout my dissertation, I interviewed "Rev. Dr. Steve," now serving as a minister in a progressive church. He was reflecting upon the time he "came out," and would tell me a peer handed him a copy of a pamphlet that was for "evangelicals who didn't want to be gay." Rev. Steve read ten pages before realizing the pamphlet was "inappropriate." His word choice was interesting to me. He did not say the pamphlet was disgusting, morally reprehensible, or offensive, but simply indicated it was not for him.

I'm saddened to see such pamphlets, as it shows to me people of faith are seeking to radically alter who God has made some to be. It also shows a misunderstanding of scripture, but, perhaps most cruelly, it destroys the confidence (however minimal they could muster) that it took to "come out." Those who never face this task do not know the toll.

In my syllabi, I remind students (queer and straight) that some have "come out," some are not yet "out," and some will never know what it's like to "come out." Therefore, Rev. Steve's use of the word "inappropriate" is remarkable to me. It's the kindest word I can think of, but perhaps he is a kinder man than I.

To the "straight church," parents, and family, you will never know what it's like to "come out." It's an incredible burden that I'm grateful you do not face, though I'm still confused why it's expected of queer people (hence the continued quotation marks). While I'd never take away my queerness, "coming out" is a task I'd undo any day.

In Search of Authentic Queer Worship

To those somehow linked to queer people, you must show compassion. While my research participant, "Wes," was grateful for some minimal support from his family, he worries what they are teaching their children. Straight family members, you had better make sure you know enough to teach your children about LGBTQ+ identities beyond insisting you don't like them. You are harming multiple lives by continuing the ignorance in your own lives, spreading it to your children, and sowing dissent and an attitude of superiority in your assumed straight children toward your queer relatives. God forbid you create the posture in your children that God cannot love the beloved in your family. How heretical to God's nature and a danger to your children and loved ones.

Most importantly, educate yourself, ask questions, and, if your faith is important to you, now is the time to show it. Otherwise, it's no wonder I'm writing this book to combat your (I'm sure, previously held) philosophies. Oh, and on that note . . . let your queer loved one see you try and make a mistake. There's nothing like ignoring a profound, earth-shaking revelation and desperately trying to move on. Your intentions may be good, but they're devastatingly harmful. It's a good and holy thing to show your love toward the identities that God has created and to those your loved ones have recently discovered. It is an affront to God otherwise. Take your time if you must—truly, only if you must—but be reminded not to lean into the chaos you're feeling before asking your loved one what they're experiencing.

One: May our apprehension bring resilience.

All: We claim the shadow of Ash Wednesday—for humanity, while a gift from You, can be so much to bear.

One: Teach us to listen, to learn, to share openly, to listen empathetically, unselfishly, and fully—never simply waiting to interject and speak.

All: For one's life may depend on our learning and listening.

"The Lord is my shepherd and He knows I'm gay." While this will be the only time you see me reference gender for the Almighty, I'm referring here to one of Rev. Troy Perry's, the founder of the Metropolitan Community Church (a haven for LGBTQ+ peoples), oft-used taglines. The same title would become the name of his book, which I own. Try reading these . . . The Lord is my shepherd and knows I'm bisexual. The Lord restores my trans soul. The Lord is preparing a table for me, a nonbinary guest. The Lord anoints my head, my queer head. Ultimately, I will dwell in the house of the Lord, known. Painful and strange as it may be, the hush of who we are will only be found on this earth, and not in heaven. Who is that family member whispering about? What are they stuttering, trying to say so quietly? Who are they trying to keep a secret from? You? You know about your own self. It isn't God! For the Lord is your shepherd, and has created you—known.

Uniting God, I feel like two different people. I'm exhausted; I'm anxious. I am, as now, seeking to be me, but I'm also who my loved ones had always known me. Unite my selves in Your time but allow me the grace of preparation. Go before my family, my friends. Fill them with compassion—may they know Your gift to me is not meant to be avoided in conversation. And if there would be a delay, may they know I seek to protect them. With understanding, may there be direct requests for clarity, but, above all, love. May that which they don't understand be met with compassion. Increase our love toward one another and you. "Teach [us] to love . . . as Thine angels love." Amen.

Omniscient One, somewhere a well-meaning person of a different variety of faith is likely praying for me. I'll take it, God. Why are they praying for me? Are they praying for my happiness, my healing from an illness, the health of my family and friends? Bless them! Are they praying for my mental health, the strength for a new day? Amen. I fear, however, they are praying that I find a perspective that I was never meant to have. Why, Giver of Love? A love that excludes? One that permits only some of Your children to be created in Your image? One that insists rationality be ignored as we interpret Your sacred text for our modern world? No, I pray for them. I pray that they see the way of love. That the sacredness of Your word would be seen through all our senses. You reward an open mind, for You have created us for it. I pray that You would enable them to see our texts both throughout history and today. I am loved by You, and you have created me in Your image. My existence is blessed just as theirs. May this be known throughout their life and mine. Amen.

∼

"I don't have friends like me" is something I have so often heard. Truthfully, I have said this myself more than once, but more often I have heard this as a partner, an academic, and a trusted confidant. This loneliness may be intentional, as an exclusionary sabotage from those showing their displeasure with us, but it may also be accidental. Friends and family may not understand, or, in many cases, may not wish to offend—and so they do not speak. They do not address an identity that is at the core of who we are. It hurts deeply. Queer spaces, virtual included, might make all the difference for your mental and emotional health. Of course, you are not alone. You join with Brok and I, the readers, and our Loving God in queer, faithful community.

ABIDE WITH ME

Abide with me: fast falls the eventide. The darkness deepens; Lord, with me abide. When other helpers fail and comforts flee, Help of the helpless, O abide with me.

— Henry Francis Lyte

I was on a train when it tragically hit someone. I later learned the person had been killed. Consequently, there was one announcement. We sat for a while, and people seemed annoyed, though I gallantly fought that same feeling with mixed success. I was struck by this emotionless display at a loss of life. I texted a friend and shared I was struggling with this display of nuisance by the general public. My friend called it "puritanical" and not overly uncommon. Someone had died, and we wondered what would become of our routine. I pray that our final moments aren't an inconvenience to someone. And, if they are, forgive them just as we needed to be forgiven in this moment. What has become society that a loss has to be quantified by how much of a factor it was for our lives? I didn't know this person, but I was involved in their death . . . by default. I wondered what had happened in our lives, in our childhood, that we were annoyed at death. I was somehow proud of myself for fighting the feeling. At least it wasn't overt, I suppose.

Was this rigidity or confusion over life and conflicting emotions the same people feel when we can't fit things (or identities) into a neat pile or category? Some were late for a scheduled meeting or a routine dinner. Someone was dead. Routine was interrupted; the ordinary was disturbed by dark death. What happens when routine is disrupted by light, by something positive? Consider such an ordinary scenario. There is no file that can fit a piece of paper that is too long. Maybe it gets its own unique spot? A better spot? You can't find a sock, so you have a novel opportunity to choose socks to show your thoughtfulness and personality. Allow yourself space to recognize where society has taught you to be "puritanical" and allow light to disrupt. Queer people have been doing that for ages; dig deep—it's there.

Eternal Light, teach us when to live in to routine, and when to break out. Most especially, teach Your people to be moldable, avoid emotional callouses, and be ready to grieve or celebrate with our siblings when emotions find us on the train or elsewhere.

3

Prayers for Community and Allies

HORACE FOUND HIMSELF IN *a fundamentalist, dangerous environment, claiming those looking to uncover his truth could "smell the gay." He was referring to the fear he had that others would be able to tell he was gay because of certain mannerisms, etc. By contrast, I was speaking at a conference with a gay colleague a couple of years ago. He immediately saw me, ran to show me his shoes, and said, "Are these too much?" It was almost as if he regretted that question when he asked. He responded by answering his own question and suggesting that's something queer people ask ourselves all the time. While we know queerness comes in so many different expressions, some of us feel unsafe or unsure to show our own brand. For queer people of faith who are fortunate to feel safe enough to express ourselves comfortably, we give thanks when others can "smell" queerness on us. What an opportunity we have to share a love that is unfathomable, and for the often-sought-after queer community that arises. Our Creator made the world in vivid colors just as all beloved creation is unique, colorful, contextual, and recognizable.*

Loving God, You have made us in community with each other. You allowed us the excitement, the fun, and the celebration to express our personalities in our own unique way for this unique time. We thank You for the community we have with our queer siblings, some we know, some we don't, and some we will. Thank You for the opportunities we have to share Your joy. When others "smell" us, may our smell be a gift, drawing us into further community with one another. For those who cannot yet be themselves, keep them safe; may they be allowed the same affordances so many of us have. Amen.

In loving memory of Flip, who I first came out to, and Kona, an incredible canine ally. In honor of Bagel, a great ally, and Cap, who's trying.

Creator, Your church sometimes feels uneasy when one prays for their beloved pet. Why? Our pets are Your creation, and we dismantle the gatekeeping of prayer permission. If we have experienced the tragic loss of a pet, our grief is real. If we are honest, it may be more genuine than the grief we have expressed over the loss of some humans. Our pets have loved us, cared for us, protected us, and provided unconditional love—now their hard work is finished. We praise You for them. They, too, are Your beloved creation, and You grieve with us. You grieve because we grieve. Give us strength, not to forget—we pray we never forget the love of such beautiful creation—but to be thankful, to be thankful You provided us with another taste of unconditional love. May this beloved pet be a model for us as we seek to love others. In time, may we find another beloved pet to carry on the tradition of mutual care for Your beloved creation. Draw us to those who will provide comfort to us. Amen.

I'm so grateful for my best friend. She now lives hundreds of miles away from me, and we make every attempt to see each other often. We're often met with comments like, "Are you two siblings?" It's almost like the bottled-up silliness bubbles over once we're together in person. As Epicurus once said, "It is not so much our friends' help that helps us, as the confidence of their help." I've never doubted she

would be there, whether it was in Illinois for a nerve-wracking dissertation defense or through life-altering mental and physical health distresses. Friendship was never meant to be conditional.

A BLESSING ON OUR FRIENDS

Friend to all, so often our friends are closer than our families. Family may not necessarily rush to sit next to us at Christmas dinner. Our friends will. Bless our friends, the friend who celebrates a newfound identity, who understands the importance of pronouns, or who commits to understanding. Our friends who join us at Pride as siblings or in solidarity. It isn't an accident we have found these friends, as surely queer people recognize these as our chosen family. We name them, we thank them, and we thank You. We ask Your blessings on them; we ask that You strengthen our relationships together. They are connections as bold, as loving, as silly, and as meaningful as always. Amen.

Holy One, we celebrate our queer siblings all around us, some timid, some bold, and many in sacred positions. While through You all is sacred, You are indeed doing a new thing. We believe that You are using queer people to show Your extravagant and overflowing, radical love to those who need to see it the most: those who seek to limit You, those who seek to limit love, and those who seek to police the limits of Your being and our calling. Forgive Your church for creating heretical limitations. Allow us new and innovative ways to worship within Your sacred tradition. As You call us and prepare us, equip us in succession to the next thing. We're ready. You prepare us through our identity in a way that has allowed us to be called to supreme and holy challenges. We're ready. Go before us, go with us, and go after us. Most of all, ensure that we never doubt our calling. To those who have not believed in our sacred duty—forgive them. Draw them to us, and draw them to Your love, so that we might foster a holy connection. You are doing a new thing, and we are privileged people. Amen.

A PRAYER FOR A QUEER INITIATIVE

Innovating God, how we give You thanks for those who have faithfully worked to ensure your beloved queer people have a safe, affirming place where they know that they are loved. We give You thanks for those who will come, who may come, and who wanted to come. We ask that this place be intentionally welcoming. May Your people be true allies, that Your love would fill the space now. We ask that those who come in support would be enthusiastically cognizant to intentionally honor the identities of all in attendance. This must be a safe space for Your people. For those who lead, give them holy wisdom as to best care. Help them to take any and all opportunities to be welcoming and kind—proving the church can, sometimes, be trusted as true ambassadors of Your love. When we fail in this regard, prompt any, immediately, to gently seek forgiveness. Bless this initiative; may it prosper. And, if not, may we never stop trying. May this truly be the means for Your church to be the embodiment of You, who is love. Amen.

I interviewed someone by the name of "Kevin," who was gay and lived in a very rural, conversative area. He was part of a non-affirming church, attending a non-affirming college. I loved talking to Kevin. His personality and candor reminded me so much of myself. When learning of terrible discrimination at a sister institution, Kevin asked his college president if he was wanted at the institution. The president responded, "You are wanted, you are loved here." This is a lovely sentiment, yes, though knowing what I know, I absolutely would have had some follow-up questions.

Students are aware of Kevin's identity, and it does not seem to be of great significance. He did indicate he had seen a few point and exclaim, "That's the gay kid." Kevin is comfortable with his label, and shared church leaders have asked him how they can do better. Kevin feels compelled to be at the institution to make it a more inclusive institution. This emotional and noble decision doesn't mean it has never been lonely or painful. Kevin would hear language such as "the family was under attack." He would ask straight people if they had heard this tagline and no one said they had, but all the queer students had noticed. I'm not overly surprised. Regardless, to Kevin, this type of language was especially poignant, as he desperately wanted a family and wanted to find love.

Kevin and I laughed when he rightfully shared how straight people receive instructions on how to do love. He said, "I don't have an instruction manual," yet elaborated by suggesting such beauty can come from writing your own manual on how to do love and realizing there are no expectations. Referencing the institutional expectations of heterosexual marriages/marriages, he compared his love freedom to a compass: "We can do anything we want," he said, likening his future path to a Lego set without instructions. As we ended our interview, we both felt as though we could have talked for hours. Kevin concluded by expressing he had never before felt he could be gay and Christian.

Abiding Love, there is no instruction manual for our relationships. Some of Your children can craft beautiful relationships creative and clever, and others need supports some of us already have. The hush accompanying our presence so often comes from the discomfort of those around us. As we progress through life, how do we now find added loneliness as a curse to overcome? Give us strength to go beyond our comfort level when we are able, but, most importantly, give a push to those in our circle. A sacred push that, through nervousness and perhaps discomfort, would allow community to be built. Bring those in our life that will care for us in the same way that we wish to care for them. You have told us that it is not good for us to be alone. May we comfort and be comforted alike. Amen.

4

Prayers of Reconciliation and Forgiveness

YEARS AGO, I TOOK *a job working for a small, divided church, and I was invited to a picnic. I did not want to go. I did and I begged Brok to go with me. He reluctantly went. I glad-handed like a politician, smiled, and ate plenty of average food. The next time I saw these people, they asked me about it. I said the food was great, and in an effort to make a bad joke said, "It must be the pagans that can't cook." Most of the people in attendance laughed at my bad joke except one man. The same man who, along with his wife, would later tell me I was a source of destruction. With all sincerity he said aloud, "I guess I'm one of those pagans."*

Bridge-building God, we sometimes become so hardened we do not hear ourselves—or worse, we do and we don't care. Humor is a gift from You, and we recognize that sometimes seeing one's face brings about strong emotion. While we cannot claim to be above our own emotions, help us to be open to new philosophies and the people behind them. Convict us in grace when we feel compelled to enter conversation, but ensure our actions are honorable. Help us to take inventory of our emotions periodically. When there is deep-seated anger, help us to identify and make amends. When amends cannot be made, may we strive for peace in all other areas of our lives—seeking to live authentically in Your love. Amen.

Healing God, this prayer is specifically for our relationships with our families. This prayer isn't detailed since so many queer people have complicated relationships with their families, and it cannot begin to describe all of ours. Offer forgiveness when necessary—to us, to them. Sometimes we avoid family or certain family as we can't bear regressing in the progress we have made. Perhaps they don't understand Your all-inclusive love, or they don't understand our identities. It may be exhausting to constantly correct names, pronouns, theology even . . . When intentions are good, may they know they are loved. Bring us together, when possible, when safe, and when reconciliation is capable. Bring those who will loudly support us into our presence. Amen.

This is the last time you'll see me mention Mollenkott's (2000) essay (probably), but I love this perspective:

> I once heard an American Baptist minister preach a powerful sermon about the importance of absolute truthfulness because God hates and punishes liars. Afterwards, I asked the preacher whether he was aware of various lies that according to scripture had received God's blessing: for instance, the Egyptian mid-wives' lying to the pharaoh (Exod 1:18–22) or the tricky deviousness of Miriam and her mother in hiding their relationship to Moses, the baby in the bulrushes (Exod 2:1–10). Following the pharaoh's order to throw all boy babies into the river, they did that but first put him into a basket that would float! With obvious discomfort, the preacher admitted that, yes, he was aware of those lies and of the blessing of God upon the liars, but he insisted that his job was to teach people to be truthful. I pressed on: "So by leaving the Bible's ethical complexities out of your sermon, you were lying by omission, but that was okay because you did so in the service of truth?" He

nodded miserably. At the time, I could think of nothing to do but to shrug and walk away, ruefully reflecting on my own "living a lie" concerning my sexual orientation. I am completing that conversation here and now, in this article. (Mollenkott 2000, 15-16)

Have you ever been so confident, so full of conviction that you made a simple error, or forgot your own lens through which you upheld such a conviction? Take a former student for example. She was homeschooled and not necessarily thrilled with her queer professor, yours truly. Like most, I sent out an email to my students before the semester introducing myself, my work, and my passions. I welcomed them to the class and wished them a great semester. This student asked to meet with me right away. If memory recalls, we met a couple hours later. This didn't seem like we were off to a great start, but I didn't know who she was, and she didn't indicate why we were to meet. We soon met, and I was introduced to someone who was wearing extremely modest clothing—neck to ankle. I warmly welcomed her and invited her into my office.

Admittedly, assumptions were made by both of us. She expressed concerns over my work, asked several questions, and made it clear that she was both very conservative and very religious. I assured her that was no problem, I do not make my own political beliefs known, and my faith is deeply important to me. I also made it clear that any work for justice is the responsibility of liberals, conservatives, and anyone in between. After a few other barbs that I'd like to think I successfully dismantled, she left, stating, "You're actually quite nice."

Huh. I thought I was nice. Opinionated, emotional, passionate, silly even, sure—but was unkind up for grabs? Now, should this student have found me when I was writing an earlier draft after an encounter with, oh, I'm not sure, a certain committee member who challenged my work often . . . I probably wouldn't have been that "nice." I'm imperfect, sure, but what I'm getting at is this . . . I react to situations in time. I'm a contextual being; our Loving God, the Holy Scriptures as a living entity, is a contextual being. Mollenkott (2000) rightfully challenged the preacher above for being so uncompromising and preaching through the Bible in such an isolated way. What *we miss when we disengage our intellect and context as Christians, readers, and worshippers is a God who doesn't defy Godself, but demonstrates when and how to act in accordance with justice, love, and (yes, using what we humans may deem to be) tricky actions appropriate for the time. Having a difference of an educated opinion does not make you unkind.*

> One: Teach us to be contextual Christians, reacting to, not simply following, rote words, embracing living, breathing, language—going rogue, if necessary, but, most importantly, responding how You would.
>
> All: May our actions be swift, changing, appropriate, and ever-faithful.
>
> One: May we not be caught unprepared for a Godly response.
>
> All: Show us Godly responses literally, contextually, logically, and wholeheartedly.
>
> One: Thanks be to God, who allows us to engage and respond to others in so many ways of belonging—reflecting the uniqueness of our being.
>
> All: Amen.

∽

Packard (2013), citing the response of a respondent named "Josh," states, "I think the reason why Sunday morning is the most segregated hour in America is because people tend to go to churches near where they live. It's not that our churches are racist; it's that they operate within a racist structure that segregates people" (148). So, while the response to "Black lives matter" may be "all lives matter," and we know they do, Anderson and Span (2016) remind us that Black lives have not yet mattered. Williams and Cooper (2020) claim 50% of White respondents indicated racial inequality would be eradicated if Black Americans "tried harder." Remember Steve King, a radical Republican former congressman? Steve called for "an America that's just so homogenous, we all look a lot the same" (Rohac 2019).

The nationalist movement seen in the United States can also be found in India, and other nations. These movements claim false histories and commemorate fraudulent heroes and histories. Yasim (2020) reports of Hindu nationalist extremists commemorating Nathuram Godse, the assassin of Mohandas Gandhi. This distortion of the truth is a resurrecting of popular, effective tactics seen throughout history. Hindu extremist monk Yogi Adityanath proposed changing the name of Meerut to Godse City. Godse believed Gandhi to be a traitor to Hindus, to be overly peaceable to Muslims, and to have allowed Pakistan to split from India during the partition. "That line is still echoed by many Hindu nationalists who see Mr. Godse as a national hero and Gandhi as a traitor" (Yasim 2020).

President Trump's supporters intensified the claim that President Obama is a secret anti-American Muslim (West 2019). Lots of intentionally traitorous words were used in those accusations. Marjorie Taylor Greene, the controversial and, well, perplexing congresswoman from Georgia, wrote on her Twitter page in 2022, "I am being attacked by the godless left because I said I'm a proud Christian Nationalist" (Lee 2022). Of greatest consequence is the co-mingling of an evangelical, far-right, self-serving crafted version of Christianity and the Republican party. Trump claims, "Christianity is under tremendous siege, whether we want to talk about it or we don't want to talk about it . . . and yet we don't exert the power that we should have . . . Christianity will have power . . . If I'm there, you're going to have plenty of power, you don't need anybody else. You're going to have somebody representing you very, very well. Remember that" (Dias 2020). Trump's words nearly imply one must profess his version of Christianity, and by default this constitutes a vote for him.

Let's sum up. In the name of religion, we want people made in God's image to look the same, show no contempt for the sin of racism, praise and celebrate murders, and use religion to provoke, agitate, and warmonger for votes. And now the peace that could come with embracing faith is defined by such vitriol and hate? When we combine politics and religion, disaster strikes, and what devastates me most is people of faith fall for it often. This heresy is such a similar mentality to that of the crusades. Those non-nationalist Christians

In Search of Authentic Queer Worship

(or people of faith) can sometimes be seen as traitors by those who are Christian nationalists. When we weaponize marginalized people, we rewrite history, which develops contempt for people who need compassion and grace the most. Look at YouTube comments on a video with a queer or trans character, and God forbid one is an educator or clergy member—a person of influence. How many of the comments cry indoctrination? It's almost as if it's a compulsion, or a fun game for self-knighted zealots. So, as if I were screaming, I remind us we are not Christian soldiers and we are not marching to war.

True Church, we await Your peace forevermore. Through toil of our own making, allow us the honor of continuing, purifying, and rethinking what we perceive as Your holy church. This isn't it. And, God, it's us to blame. Amen.

∽

I learn so much hearing Rabbi Angela Buchdahl of Central Synagogue in New York City speak. Her candor, compassion, and intelligence helps to ground me in my understanding of my faith. Paraphrasing aspects of a previous Yom Kippur sermon (2024), she shared when we hold someone in high esteem and we see them stumble, we rarely provide grace as much as we account their wrong as their "true character." Imagine thinking, could I have been so mistaken about this person? Rabbi Buchdahl suggests, without remorse, forgiveness may not be a requirement, but imagine the toll of disrepair for ourselves. Additionally, consider the anxiety we may bear, and the fear we ourselves may experience as our society seems to be one of zero chances. I encourage you, call in whenever possible—minding your own self, capabilities, and mental health. "Whenever" is the poignant word. "Whenever" may sometimes indicate not here, not now. Yet, may it be our personal custom and philosophy.

Pursuing Redeemer, You lovingly chase after us. Our account, like so many of our beloved heroes, will be mixed with the good and the bad. There will be no perfection. How quick we are to expect forgiveness for our actions, yet we linger when others have wronged us. The wrong may be hateful, and perhaps we sit, pray, and ask for Your care for our next steps. It may be dangerous for a select few to remain a part of our lives. Whenever possible, may calling in and forgiveness be our custom. When there is misunderstanding or no understanding, give us grace to recognize that fear of offense and personal communication so often keep us from healthy dialogue. Help us to avoid making judgment calls, claiming one-time actions to be one's "true character." Give us grace, give them grace—yet may we avoid creating us versus them in favor of allowing us and them to be in dialogue whenever possible. Amen.

5

Prayers of Resistance and Justice

ONE OF MY FAVORITE classes I took in my doctoral career was a course on queer theory. The professor was silly, outrageously intelligent, and very informal. I had written a research proposal that I was rather proud of, and we were meeting individually to discuss it. She read it, nodded repeatedly and continually, and said, "It's too clean. You need to get messier." Granted, this was one of the last classes I took before the dissertation stage, and I don't know that she was going to change everything I had learned in that short time we had together. I tried to be messier, but every time we met, she would say the same thing. My work was too clinical? Maybe it made too much sense? Maybe it wasn't ambitious enough, or perhaps it had been done before? Friends, while I had relatively failed there, where do you see opportunities to be messier? In your personal life or professional life, or perhaps in your spiritual life? Perhaps it's supporting an initiative, or being brave socially or with your mental health. Perhaps offering suggestions may not make sense, which might be the start of my being messy. Yet, whenever possible, queer (used as a verb here) corners of your life that have nothing to do with your identity. Stretch, reach, apply new things to otherwise unheard-of solutions. Our God is limitless; give limitless a try.

Sacred Instigator, ignite in us an unquenchable passion for things beyond our imagination. Give us the power to ignore with holy graciousness, should attempts be made to place boundaries on what is capable through our work together. Make us messy people who do messy work and crave a messy purpose. Amen.

I'm not a trans person, but I love one. I'm friends with many and will stand with all. I find myself writing this upon hearing about a deeply offensive event some in my community were involved with, which caused me to do some reflection. Queer people have so much that unites us, but our stories can dramatically vary across bodies, identities, demographics, abilities, personalities, and race. In some ways, what unites us is rejection. Sometimes that is rejection from society, but also choosing to reject society-enforced labels. God has created us to reject things that were never intended. In a way, our Creator has made us "extra free." Society didn't like that, as the patriarchal ties that bind would then have had to be loosened. Trans people are not political or spiritual pawns. The love God has for trans people, those whom the Almighty has created to defy societal oppressors, is a gift—an incredibly challenging gift. Jesus came to defy oppressors. Director and advocate Janet Mock (2014) comments, "I believe that telling our stories, first to ourselves and then to one another and the world, is a revolutionary act. It is an act that can be met with hostility, exclusion, and violence. It can also lead to love, understanding, transcendence, and community."

As Kevin, who I spoke with earlier, would tell me, he believed LGBTQ+ people were put on this earth to show others how to love. Drawing from Rev. Gary David Comstock's Gay Theology Without Apology *(1993), we look to the story of Queen Vashti in the Book of Esther. Vashti is summoned before the King, and she refuses to come. She refuses her label of subservience. She is killed for this choice. Perhaps she preferred the company of her friends or she had the common sense not to appear before a drunken king who wanted her to display herself. Regardless, she refused to succumb to the social*

order. King Ahasuerus gives a proclamation that all women are to give honor to their husbands, "a striking and poignant illustration of patriarchal panic!" (Comstock 1993).

> *In lifting up her little-known or ignored story—in bringing it in from the margin to the center—in rewriting her story in our actions today, we use the Bible as a resource for moral agency, for making things better, for making justice. Instead of looking to the Bible for answers that can be copies to solve today's problems, instead of trying to copy what is done in the Bible, our confrontation with the Bible becomes a model for confronting the moral dilemmas we face in our lives today. (Comstock 1993, 57)*

Make us Vashtis. Disruptors. Allowing our ordinary, yet far from ordinary, daily life to change the social order. Help us to live into our God-created role as courageous revolutionaries. Amen.

∽

Anderson and Span (2016) remind us that White people living in U.S. counties that had high concentrations of slaves in 1860 remain more conservative and tend to harbor colder feelings toward Black Americans compared to White people in other southern regions. This legacy suggests that White America is still struggling to fully embrace Black Americans as part of their community. Such a segregated identity is embedded in various societal structures. Remember the words of "Josh"? "The reason Sunday morning is the most segregated hour in America is because people tend to go to churches near where they live. It's not that our churches are racist; it's that they operate within a racist structure that segregates people."

Can we divorce our worship from our surroundings, O God? If we could, why would we choose to? When we are aware of where we worship, and who our neighbor is—how they look, love, and believe—only then do we live in community with our siblings. Teach us to give attention to lives that haven't historically mattered and teach us to say this without it, metaphorically, burning our tongue.

For surely You aren't thinking about trivial things when you see us cross the street to avoid your beloved. You prod us to action. Following Your example, You give us an opportunity to disrupt the bigoted social order of our own making. You teach us that while all of Your children are important, in this moment, that one in need of restoration is the one that should have our focus. Why can't Your church do the same? Your queer and trans children, Your Black children. Or, God, perhaps it is Your children who are lonely, those in need of mental health care. Isn't it inevitable that some of our neighbors will need more of our attention at specific times? Forgive us for our insensitivity and foolishness. Amen.

❖ ❖ ❖

"God of Abraham, praise": This we ask of our queer siblings around the world—many in this country, where political turmoil and propaganda have caused some to believe queer lives to be thought of as expendable. Give us agency, community, and allies who vote with a research-backed and faith-filled conscience. To those who long for visibility and representation, give courage and conviction. To those ruled by dangerous leaders, give protection, liberty, and freedom. May people of faith lead this endeavor. To those riddled with anxiety in body, mind, and spirit, awaiting news of conflicting election results, give peace. For (leader's name), give authority and confidence to stand with even the most marginalized of citizens. Where violence reigns and scapegoats are sought, may citizens see through facades. To those whose eyes are still closed, open them, and quickly. Awaken their intellect, awaken their faith. Amen.

Martin Luther King Jr. (1967), citing the words of Hyman Bookbinder, suggests a sacrifice of the privileged must occur in the name of equality. In 2005, Wantland wrote about a successful scenario in which fraternity men were tasked with taking part in a cohort-style gender studies course. Upon the successful completion of the course, a male student, when accidentally meeting a teaching assistant, exclaimed he could not have sex with an intoxicated woman because "this class gave me fucking morals." Another scenario . . . one of the

men blurted aloud, "That's so gay." The other male students proved offended and glared, and the student quickly apologized.

I suspect a few of us had a strong image in our heads conjured when I mentioned fraternity men. In many cases, these are privileged, straight, wealthy, White men. Not always, of course, though perhaps the very ones that King and Bookbinder suggest could be an asset to those in need of an ally. This experiment ultimately proved to be a situation where I suspect many perfectly lovely men benefited from education and found themselves supporting their siblings. Now, their environment was controlled, free of so many outside influences, but given that particular environment, this is also why I cringe when some say "I just don't understand" when one "comes out."

Craig et al. (2017) share a research participant's words: "I eventually left and no longer consider myself Catholic or a member of any organized religion. I still long for the sense of community I experienced and would love connecting with other [LGBTQ] former members of religious orders." I am devastated by the apparent cost-benefit analysis that seems to be occurring here. I suppose it makes sense to lose a few, remove them from the community, rather than have them succumb to the "sin" of their identity under the watchful eye of a clergy member. Of course, I am being sarcastic, but the prayers of a queer one's longing for community were loudly heard by God. Those who repeatedly turned them away will have some questions to answer, undoubtedly.

I had an 80-year-old gentleman audit two courses with me. He was a former mental health professional turned clergy member. A thoughtful man, who was kind, lovely, and a tremendous influence on the others—myself included. He was grateful to return to class many decades later to reconsider his role in society, the value he might have on this generation, and how we might consider ways of interpreting valuable material. He understood what to do during times of change. Thank you, my friend.

> O that now the church were blest
> With faith and faith's increase!
> Grant us, Lord, the outward rest
> And true internal peace;

> Build us up in holy love,
> And let us walk with God below,
> Serve thee as thy hosts above,
> And all thy comfort know.
> — CHARLES WESLEY

During my dissertation stage, I interviewed Professor Cynthia. Professor Cynthia was unlike the others, a progressive Christian who only found herself at this conservative university since it was near her ailing mother. An artist by trade, she felt tension due to her beliefs, as her colleagues would say things like, "How could you go there?," "Please don't ask me to exhibit there," "They hate homosexuals," "[This is the] college with weirdos." At one point, she invited a Jewish organization to attend a show, and they were surprised and almost fearful to have been invited to the institution. I asked her the same question and she responded in a beautiful, meaningful way, replying, "[This institution] needs people like me who will be more embracing of Christ's love. So I stay." "So I stay" may be the most powerful words spoken in my presence. This suggests she was willing to deal with her own discomfort, negotiate her convictions to be the loving, affirming presence in the face of a radical environment. There is a time to leave, yes, a time for change, but how important it may be also to stay. For a radical extrovert with severe ADHD who craves change, the next sentence is terribly hard to write. Here it goes ... When might you have reason to center yourself, take a deep breath, and think, "So [I'll] stay"?

> One: In Ecclesiastes 3, the author reminds of the constant changes in life: "For everything there is a season, and a time for every matter under heaven."
>
> All: Our lives are constantly in flux, unsettling to some, exciting to others.
>
> One: The seasons of change call us to consider the connotation of God's prodding, a nudge from a sacred text, a response to a beloved community ...
>
> All: In the seasons of life, we respond differently during times of grief, celebration, and anger, during highs and great lows in life.

One: While change is inevitable, God reminds us there is a time to go, yet we consider if we might be too quick to go.

All: The beauty of ancient wisdom and rituals keep alive this beautiful faith that leaves space for discernment.

One: Praise be to the One who gives us the discernment to stay or go.

All: Remind us that neither is a means of surrender.

One: Give us strength to forcibly, radically be a guiding light, a headlight on a dangerous curve, protecting us and others from danger. If we stay, accompanying this decision is the insistence to avoid conforming. We must always speak, calling out injustice. For this is the duty of those who stay.

All: And if we go . . .

One: If we go, allow us "a time to break down, and a time to build up."

All: So be it. Amen.

One: Your message of peace has so frequently been stolen by a misplaced, tokenized version of masculinity and angry people of faith.

All: Teach us Your way on earth is not by conquering, but by service and humility.

One: Generations later, forgive us the sin of misunderstanding Your entry into Jerusalem.

All: You ride on a humble donkey, showing Your vulnerability. Standing with the poor, You destroy systems of inequality in the temple.

One: Dona nobis pacem.

All: We are not Christian soldiers. We are not marching to war.

One: Grant us peace. Grant us peace.

All: Amen.

A PRAYER OF CHRIST'S HUMILITY

Ride on, ride on in majesty! In lowly pomp ride on to die, bow Your meek head to mortal pain, then take, O Christ, Your pow'r and reign. Amen.

—Henry H. Milman

Reclaiming God, we join You to celebrate in unity. Queer people have so often been forced to reclaim that which is hurtful. We celebrate the resilience that You have given to us to reclaim the past. Your cross, we reclaim. We wear it around our necks, we bow in Your church, we make the sign of Your holy cross in reverence and celebration. This symbol of torturous death—a mockery. We reclaim. This symbol of pain, of public humiliation, is a symbol of devotion of undying love to Your people. May that which is meant to mock, humiliate, hate, and denigrate be reclaimed. Teach us to reclaim. Amen.

6

Prayers of Celebration and Joy

BLESS, O GOD, THIS life-affirming, sustaining substance (medication, hormones, etc); may I use this substance to further embrace who You have created me to be. Meet my excitement and anxiety and allow me to embrace both as valid. When and if I am able, may I return my gratitude to others who need my care, love, support, and strength. Use my willingness to give encouragement to queer people who may see none. Amen.

A PRAYER FOR THE DAY OF GENDER AFFIRMATION SURGERY

"Welcome, happy morning!" With gratitude, I thank You. Today is a new day. I have awaited this day to bring me nearer to Your plans for me. Though I come with euphoria, I come also with nervousness. Yes, the usual medical anxiety, but mostly the after. Will people ignore me, will they be dismissive, looking for reasons to avoid using my name or identity? Still, I follow who I am. This child of God follows unashamedly forward to the territory to which most have not been called. May those, for whom this is not their calling, be my strength, my companion, my ally, and my friend. Amen.

A PRAYER FOR A PRIDE CELEBRATION

Loving God, forgive and change the hearts of those who seek to harm us on this day, for You are with us in joyful celebration. We praise You for those people of faith, allies, and supportive friends, old and new, who will join on this celebratory day. Empower us to ignore those who spew hatred. May this community join in sacred bonds to show love, grace, and radical acceptance. On this day, societal labels and rigid norms mean little. Joy, happiness, and boldness reign. On this day, we make new friends and celebrate our shared identities. Through all our deserved fun, may we not forget to give thanks to You for creating us in such a beautiful, unique way. May our world follow Your example of recognizing our uniqueness as a special creation. Amen.

～

God of Love, you are Love, your love knows no boundaries, it knows no conditions, it embraces all your children. We pray for communities of love and inclusion where no one is judged by the demands and expectations of others but called to love as you love. As we celebrate Pride Month, enable us to see every human being as a child made in your image and whose life is to be blessed with compassion, love, kindness, respect, and dignity, for this is your way and this is your will.

—The Cathedral Church of St. James, The Anglican Church of Canada *(used with permission)*

～

The most sacred place in the world to me is the National Cathedral in Washington, D.C. I go frequently. Brok woke me up early a few years ago—a cold, November morning, telling me all kinds of lies to get me there before the sunrise. It was our anniversary and he wanted us to have our picture taken as the sun rose over this holy place. It holds particular meaning for me, as it was the first place where I heard a queer clergyperson preach. Admittedly, I also used it as a means for me to escape my very conservative church on that particular Sunday. From that day, I understood that God loves queer people. I can easily draw a straight line from a seemingly random Sunday in my early years to the present and any future work. The moment set me on a direct path to uncovering the truth behind the Holy Scriptures, the sacredness of God's unfathomable love, and the means of worship where all are truly invited, valued, and incorporated into God's holy church. The impact of the representation was incomprehensible.

> Draw the circle, draw the circle wide. Draw the circle, draw the circle wide.
> No one stands alone, we'll stand side by side. Draw the circle, draw the circle wide.
> Draw the circle wide, draw it wider still. Let this be our song: no one stands alone. Standing side by side, draw the circle, draw the circle wide.
> — Words by Gordon Light, (c) 1994, Common Cup Music Society, commoncup.com

∼

One: On this day, we give thanks for those saints who, through holy justice, resisted, argued, lovingly conversed, and practiced your sacraments.

Many: "For all the saints."

One: We thank You for those who cared, comforted, loved, guided, and supported these efforts when all seemed fruitless.

Many: "For all the saints."

One: We stand in Your broken church as tired people, smiling, but exhausted, thankful, but wounded. We recall times spent waiting in cars, parking lots, lobbies, seeking courage to enter Your church—recognizing all have not indeed been welcoming.

Many: "But then there breaks a still more glorious day." Alleluia!

One: On this new day, take risks for the sake of the illumined church and our fearless God in the inclusive orthodoxy God has ordained since Pentecost. "Be a sinner and sin boldly."

Many: "But let Your trust in Christ be stronger and rejoice in Christ who is the victor over sin, death, and the world."

All: Amen.

These are the two prayers we prayed the night before Brok's surgery:

Help me, Creator God, to resist the temptation to be what I am not. Let me be me—as you have created me. Help me to enjoy the blessings in my own yard, knowing that they are very good indeed.

—Donna E. Schaper *(used with permission)*

I am a loveable, creative person made in the likeness of God. I give myself permission to enjoy being myself to love without fear of rejection, to create with imagination, to change without dread of the future, to use my power responsibly, to work for justice and peace
And live as a singer and dancer within God's all embracing being.

—W. L. Wallace *(used with permission)*

7

Prayers for the Sanctity and Restoration of the Church

LOVING GOD, SOMETIMES WE enter Your church joyfully, sometimes begrudgingly; sometimes we look for excuses to leave Your sanctuary, and we promise we will arbitrarily make it up to You—though we may or may not. You know us, so You know that this has much more to do with Your church than it does being in communion with You. Hearing confused or misguided people who try to explain to us how we are to use the identities You've given us, hearing clergy entrusted to us woefully confuse or avoid queer issues, and then, of course, wondering if allies or friends will support us in context. While we know You don't need a church to reveal Your love to us, You call us to Your church. Give us grace and patience, especially lead us to where You would have us worship and be in community with loving people. Remind us that we are not heretics if we call for reform in Your church. We draw from the aspirational words of Charles Wesley's ascension hymn, "Blessings on [God's] church below, Alleluia!" We see this as a call for radical reconciliation within a deeply flawed and divided church. Amen.

Early in my career in academia, I was teaching a rather uncontroversial class. I joked it was to justify my job. I had a lovely student in that class, and, while we both cared for each other, it was clear we differed on many ideas. There were some strong debates, yet all were respectful. He came to my office one day and gave me one of the biggest surprises I had received in my career. He shared with me that he would be registering for a class I taught on sexuality. This was most certainly not an uncontroversial course. He knew this; he whispered it to me. I informed him that he would be welcome, and, while I was surprised, I was glad he would be in my class. He shared with me he wanted to understand if what he had been taught and believed for many years was grounded in research and accurate. Essentially, is this "disputable"? It wasn't necessarily an easy class for me that semester, yet how amazing the world would be if we had more people who adopted a similar attitude?

"Professor Bill," one of my research participants, sympathetically used the term "disputable theology." A theology professor in a fundamentalist institution, he was a low-grade, conservative theological troublemaker. He advised (queer) students to be true to themselves, think carefully, and allow moral convictions to be shaped by scripture. He likened the church's moral debate over gender and sexuality to the subtext behind 1 Corinthians 8, in which the apostle Paul is discussing the permissibility of eating meat offered to idols. Professor Bill calls this "disputable theology" and argues we cannot argue over "disputable theology." He continued by stating some would say it is permissible to eat this meat. Acknowledging it may seem trivial to others, yet if placed within this context now, such a decision is no longer trivial, but a moral decision. Thinking again of context, Professor Bill states he is not a Jewish person living in the era of the apostle Paul, but if he was, now such a decision would have enormous consequences. A weaker faith would not *eat the meat, as it takes a stronger faith to say we no longer live in such an era. Professor Bill affirms, "If you want to be a prophet, be prepared to be persecuted as a prophet."*

God over confusion, You welcome our doubts and are faithful when we are not yet ready to be true to ourselves. Forgive our churches, when we are not even brave enough to whisper our advocacy or to express our desire to learn about Your children. May we always be ready to whisper love, allyship, or support—but may our whispers be very temporary. May our whispers give way to screams of confidence and passionate hospitality. May Your churches scream love and protection, and may we, Your queer beloved, increase the volume. We welcome a whisper. Amen.

∼

I was asked to present at a conference, and, when asked for a bio, I called myself a "critical Methodist." "Critical" was the kindest word I could think of at the time, shortly after the General Conference overturned the exclusionary language of LGBTQ+ peoples. "Reluctant" came to mind, too. When asked about my choice of language, these words came to mind:

God, our "hope for years to come," we praise You for those who have done this holy work before us, and those who will do so after us—though we ask that it is easier for those to come. On this day of progress, we are thankful that Your church sees Your beloved queer people as equal and valid. Forgive us if this feels insignificant. It feels inadequate and even sacrilegious for the church to place barriers on who You have called to serve Your people and how they are to love. We have not stopped proclaiming Your love. We will hear from those who speak out in disgust, calling heresy. How dare others think this places us in some hierarchically lower Christian status? While Your church has now attempted to reconcile policy with Your love and Your call, we have lost so many over the political violence of our own making. How do we recover? This self-inflicted tragedy did not have to be like this. I am critical, but I'm called—so I stay. Reflecting on the earlier war path that led us to this rightful place in history, I feel pity, admittedly anger and grief, but also sorrow. Bring those home to a place where Your all-consuming love can be found, to a place where we no longer dare to limit You. Amen.

> *Theologian Reinhold Niebuhr stated this comment, and I'll let you decide if it is fact: The church has lost the chance to become the unifying element in our American society. It is not anticipating new facts. It is merely catching up slowly to the new social facts created by economic and other forces . . . What we accomplish in the way of church unity ought to be accepted with humility and not hailed with pride. We are not creating. We are merely catching up with creation. (Niebuhr 1929, 90)*

This comment isn't necessarily untrue, I'd argue, but it's enough to make an apologist nauseous. You've seen me allude to this throughout. What is the church doing today? We are not a unifying body, certainly. In fact, the church has so often been a tremendous source of harm.

Borrowing from Liturgy and Justice: To Worship God in Spirit and Truth *(Koester 2002), "Without speaking specifically of justice, Jesus is constantly dealing with the reality . . . " The leper is not simply cured, having been ostracized from society and the synagogue; the leper is now restored to community. Jesus heals a disfigured hand on the Sabbath, to stress a right relationship with God. Jesus wasn't a vending machine of miracles, no. Jesus was a wraparound community provider, dealing with physical needs, spiritual needs, and social justice. That was a necessity to Jesus. To celebrate those in community with the church is pleasant, but it is rather performative, and mostly for those already in the church. It's awfully shortsighted—or, as Niebuhr might say, only to be accepted with humility. What an opportunity the church has missed! Forgive the church, when they intentionally avoid ministry with certain groups, peoples, illnesses, or identities.*

Back to Mollenkott (2000) (really, finally):

> During my Protestant fundamentalist childhood, I was taught that it was a Christian's responsibility to avoid even the appearance of evil (1 Thess. 5:22). It was years before it dawned on me that in Jesus' story of the good Samaritan, the two priests who refused their help to a man fallen among thieves were doing exactly that—abstaining from all appearance of evil. Had they assisted the bleeding man,

In Search of Authentic Queer Worship

they would have gotten dirt and blood on their stainless garments—and, God forbid, someone might think that they themselves had been involved in the mugging! (Mollenkott 2000, 17–18)

Such literalism is agony. Jesus wants us to get our hands dirty, and when we avoid the appearance of evil, we might just be the foolish ones who did nothing but sit on our coins, making no difference whatsoever (Luke 19).

The following selection from Gay Theology Without Apology *is one of my favorite selections of queer text. I have read it aloud to others often. Read it aloud to prove to yourself that your story is partially told, but only ever partially. Read it aloud to show others, or convince yourself, that no one "has a lock" on your Christianity. Read this now to incentivize, encourage, and remind yourself that hands with dirt on them are active hands. They have been provoked to action—so I ask you to work for a faith that begs to be embraced with curiosity:*

> *. . . answers and solutions to social problems are rarely found in the official word but can be constructed out of listening for and lifting up the silenced word. The story of Vashti has been rewritten many times, and we may continue to rewrite it. The story of Vashti was rewritten when an underground rail-road, and not complacency, was the response to a people's ignored cry for freedom; the story of Vashti was rewritten when armed resistance, and not accommodation, was the response to Hitler's program in the Warsaw Ghetto Uprising; the story of Vashti was rewritten when a boycott, and not continued obedience, was the response to the arrest of a tired woman who dared to sit down on a bus where she was not supposed to; the story of Vashti was rewritten when a few lesbians and gay men finally did not go gently into that ever-waiting paddy wagon outside the barroom door and staged the Stonewall Rebellion, the founding event of the modern lesbian/gay movement." (Comstock 1993, 57)*

In the name of our restoring God, Amen!

Convicting God, all churches do not preach, love, worship, and obey Your commands the same. Help us to discern when we are called to leave a community of faith and when to stay during times of challenge. How do I stay in communion with those who are faithful to a church that wants nothing to do with me? Those that will not consider "disputable theology"? While there may be no vindictiveness in their actions, how am I to perceive their reluctance to engage? This I offer to You. Convict them in the way of love, and not convenience. Amen.

∼

Our Jewish siblings may enter the synagogue singing "Ma Tovu." This beautiful prayer expresses reverence for the house of worship—the holy space. The prayer begins in Numbers 24:5, as Balaam is sent to curse Israel, but is instead struck in holy reverence by the dwelling of the Almighty. I'd ask that you pause to find the prayer now. Indeed, curses are turned to blessings. Spaces are made holy, and we prepare ourselves to worship by one who initially came to wish others harm.

- One: Ma Tovu (How Good), One who desires blessings, has witnessed curses, but transforms minds through the reverence and sacredness of Your divine presence and learning. You reward an open mind.
- All: Grant us grace to understand the love You have for those who wish to harm those who You love.
- One: For we have all been Balaam, and now we, too, seek blessings.
- All: The blessings found in this sacred place have come from You.
- One: There are many who have wished us ill, and we invite them to this sacred place to witness your transformation.
- All: May they, too, experience a blessing from a curse. And, if not, may they leave in peace.
- One: Some blessings are not instantaneous.
- All: We give you thanks for years of study, faithful dialogue, uncomfortable conversations that may or may not have been gratifying.

In Search of Authentic Queer Worship

One: We are Exodus people. People now of freedom, people leaving captivity, some joined nervously with another in hand, but leaving our captive entity behind.

All: Oh, How Good!

∽

Years ago, I had a student who truly confused me. I was, I think, as cordial as possible. However, she missed a week of class and asked me one day, during class, to go back and teach everything from that last week. I thought she was kidding, as did her peers. She wasn't. Is there ever a time to go back? In context—here, no. I always want to go forward, since I'm so tired of constantly explaining myself and our relationship. Brok is especially. I wrote about this once and called it "crude exposure therapy." You see, Brok in many ways is much braver than I am. I'm a cisgender person, Brok is not, and my "coming out" experience was much different. However, the thing that I love and hate about his brain, that I will never understand, is there is no going back. We lived into our identities hard. I did gradually, but significantly over twenty-odd years. Brok did (certainly over the same), but his public "coming out" process, to others that weren't me, was more like three years.

Many churches are open to queer people; many are not. Those that are, where are you going? Now that we're blessed to come (read sarcastically), what's your plan for us? Do you know the unique needs of our community, both as a community and individual members? Are you listening to us? It feels too easy to ask to go back to times when you ignored us. Not because you don't love us, but because you don't know what to do with us. Fortunately, while we've craved the church's blessing, we never needed it. I love the church, and I yearn for it to see us more clearly, but we have God's blessing. That's never changed. Thanks be to God.

I was honored to lead a talkback session after a performance of a beautiful play, The Revelation of Bobby Pritchard, *written by Maryland playwright Rich Espey. These lines feel appropriate here:*

> HANK
> *Unlock the church and open it to you for your wedding? Stand at the altar while you and her . . . Are you that crazy?*
>
> (later in the show)
>
> KATHY
> *If you soil my church on Saturday . . . if you contaminate . . .*
>
> HANK
> *Then what? What happens, Kathy? The river will keep on flowing. Just like it has flowed since creation, just like it flowed the night a good man named Bobby Pritchard died, just like it flowed forty years since, and just like it will flow to eternity.*
> *Thank you for the pie. (Espey 2015, 66, 84)*

Open wide the doors, for when we say all are welcome, anything other than "all" is blasphemous. Convicting God, restore your church. Amen.

∼

> One: Restoration is indeed orthodoxy, though orthodoxy may not yet have been seen on this earth.
>
> All: The church is community, the church is home, and the church is love. Where do we go when it isn't?
>
> One: We seek this in the ordinary. In the sacred ordinary that God allows us—viewing community in the church adjacent.
>
> All: We gave thanks for the aspiring church, and those that commit.
>
> One: To those that undertake this work, be mindful of your impact. Be ever engaged in learning. Should you commit to a community shown a mixed status about their standing within the church, this is your obligation.
>
> All: In spaces where we serve as allies, we commit to intentional learning, intentional language, and intentional listening. If

we cannot honor such a commitment, we commit to staying away until we can.

Do you find yourself internally making value judgments? Who are the most faithful people: Methodists, Lutherans, Anglicans, Presbyterians, Catholics? Maybe I'd get a truer answer if I reframed it and asked you, Who is the least faithful? Whenever I propose a compromise, or a non-permanent solution, Brok often says, "That's a Band-Aid solution." What if it is? Band-Aids are great; they cover hurt, keep out infection. I suppose Brok's worry is about digging out the root of the issue, yet mortals can rarely uncover the root of the issue and are constantly torn between finding bigger and bigger Band-Aids. I suspect if we either use or refuse to use hypothetical Band-Aids we might have to realize we are accepting some sort of inadequacy. Problems don't go away simply with temporary fixes, but we can delay them. Sometimes we need to delay a problem to focus on another, and, besides, digging relentlessly when we don't have an end goal or cannot reach the end leaves a bigger, possibly unfillable or un-healable hole. Let's acknowledge a few things. The writer of the words you've read thus far is deeply inadequate and is aligned with an imperfect religion, a beautiful one, but still, one that leaves us with many questions. We wrestle with these questions taught to us in an imperfect way, within an even more imperfect society. Ultimately, we must work to endeavor toward unity within the open confines of scripture and sacred texts.

∽

By adapting sociologist Laura Hamilton's idea of "trading on heterosexuality" (2007), the concept may give the evangelical community the ability to aggressively and affectionately show more outward affection and intimacy toward another man in their circle—platonically, of course. However, this notion can only be acceptable if there is no doubt the men are straight, and the "trading" may be excusable only if it is for entertainment and in context, to create a community of hardcore, other aligned Christian men.

Consider another view. Sociologist C. J. Pascoe's (2003) idea of "jock insurance" may be an explanation. Though the connotation is not within an athletic environment, as the world knows, evangelical men are extraordinarily heterosexual and entirely conventionally masculine; any expression otherwise can now be permissible. How can they "get away" with this, you ask? Well, the extreme expression of straightness in the sea of straight creates the opportunity to remain unscathed from the opinions of like-minded men. It almost drowns out any doubt about queerness.

The evangelical church has so often been fueled by an intense form of masculinity, which has been embodied by muscled, White men. Christian hardcore punk bands even adopt a hegemonic form of masculinity (without being too academic, we might think a toxic form of masculinity) to masculinize the church. McDowell (2017) cites a relevant blog expressing the belief that "in a nation where the men seem to be slipping away from the Church, and the church too often seems to be emasculating those who remain, this is the kind of movement that we need. We need strong men of God to carry the Church into the next generation." McDowell suggests that some individuals adapt by reimagining Christianity as more masculine, portraying Jesus as a tough, strong figure with large biceps, emphasizing strength over peace in marketing. This strategy aims to attract more White men by engaging them in spaces where they already thrive, such as gyms, sports, and concerts, ensuring that any perceived loss of complacent followers can be offset by the inclusion of like-minded, fervent White men.

We're not exactly secretive about using the Lord's name in vain. Allow me to clarify—specifically, when we insist on a view of Jesus that is wildly imaginative and one that is self-serving and harmful. This is often used so that we might gain or destroy, asserting our own ideology (particularly when it is against the very nature of who Jesus is). Somewhere in the Middle East, away in a dirty, unhygienic trough, Emmanuel awakes. But obviously, there is crying. Why? Well, because our Emmanuel is fully human, and naturally infants, even those sent from Heaven, cry and might just awaken and startle the cows. There probably weren't too many peaceful nights.

I want to take a turn. Who is your vision of Jesus? It's refreshing in some ways for me to imagine an extroverted Jesus embracing a queer identity. This Jesus will join me for frequent coffee, walking the dogs, and finding hole-in-the-wall shops. Brok's Jesus? If I may guess, This Jesus understands what it's like to live out an identity, create that identity, and embrace it—yes, nervously, but bravely. This Jesus knows who They are! Hmmmmm. Let's leave that there . . .

More practically, this Jesus loves board games (I'll never understand why), dogs, staying home (again, don't understand why), and eating candy. I know some will say that this was an offensive Jesus I asked you to consider, but I'm no heretic. Why should you be offended when, let's suppose, an African artist uses African artistry in their rendering of something sacred? That's kind of a beautiful expectation, no? The versions here are the ones that show an image of created selves. Can you find yours? What they don't do is create hostile versions that marginalize, eradicate, destroy community, and disunify. On a final note, this queer Jesus is Love and cannot be categorized—there's no other. So often have we used and we use queer as a noun; let's consider it as an adjective. To be queer is to be uncategorizable and atypical, even unexpected—I don't know, not . . . of . . . this . . . world, perhaps? I'd better end here, as perhaps I've said too much. How wonderful, my friend, to conclude with similarities of ourselves and a love that is an identity, a name, a noun, and an adjective.

Love in all forms, we have constantly asked for Your guidance that we may see ourselves. I'm not sure that we have, but perhaps we're closer than we've been. This is what we're asking and striving for—simple adjacence. We silly humans attempt to draw comparisons, and while this may be the closest we get, we're asking that it's enough to keep going. Thanks be to God who upholds and protects us from the imperfect church that has harmed. Your perfect love hovers us from the anxiety of uncertainty and uplifts us during the fear of a new thing.

Fling wide the portals of your heart; make it a temple, set apart from earthly use for heaven's employ, adorned with prayer and love and joy.

—G. Weissel

8

Conclusion

MITCHELL AND SNYDER (2014) *imply a foundational error in discussing an individual with a disability, the erasure of identity and characterization by such disability. Within the Christian scriptures, the Ethiopian eunuch is only known as such. It is as though the most important aspect of the man's identity was that he was an enslaved eunuch. Though the eunuch in scriptures is later allowed to join the church, he does so by another principle highlighted by Mitchell and Snyder. He overcomes his disability. His disability forbids him from community, relationships, and worship. Those with disabilities need not overcome such disability to celebrate humanity. In an effort to avoid the acceptance of what should be condemned, perhaps we see the Bible in context, a "period piece." We contend, and dialogue with it as a friend.*

Solevåg (2016) writes, "The story of the Ethiopian eunuch has, I would argue, the potential to locate the queer, broken, disabled body at the center of Christianity." Instead, the Norwegian Bible Society has published a new Bible that has eliminated the use of the word eunuch, further erasing the identity of an already marginalized Biblical character. The term "eunuch" is found in Norwegian as evnuk, suggesting a relevant translated word is irrelevant. This erasure, seen in Norway and beyond, suggests that a queer (in some way) man who is both physiologically asexual and maintains some level of "gender trouble" is irrelevant to Christianity. The Ethiopian eunuch, seen to exist outside of the male binary, contradicts the notion above suggesting devout Christians need only be concerned with a heteronormative, ableist, anti-queer approach to understanding scriptures and divinely given identities. For many queer Christians, the account of the eunuch suggests their theology is inclusive of their bodies and identities.

We've seen this before, however. Christians erasing or altering parts of history or sacred texts that cause discomfort is nothing new. Consider the ancient story of Lot. Toensing (2005) writes, "Instead I assert that the wickedness of these cities is the inhospitable treatment of resident aliens and sojourners at its worst, through the sexual humiliation of rape, linked with the wickedness of idolatry." The dangers of doing so are reflected in generations of queer people clamoring for representation, acknowledgement, or, at the very least, conversation. While many churches claim they affirm, the affirmation is superficial, or "welcoming" is confused with affirming. A rainbow flag may be nice to know where to begin to find community, but then what? Rainbow stoles are performative when queer people crave queer theology.

Friends,

What have you read that has remained in your consciousness? I hope this brought you peace, but, more importantly, I hope these prayers have reminded you that God has made you with love. We have always been part of the Almighty's plan. "May the Lord bless you and keep you." Remember, friends, echoing Martin Luther, "Be a sinner, and sin boldly, but let your trust in Christ be stronger."

Peace.

About the Author

DR. ERIC HESS (HE/HIM) has been an academic his entire career. He earned his doctorate from the University of Illinois, where his research emphasized queer Christianity.

References

Anderson, James D., and Christopher M. Span. 2016. "History of Education in the News: The Legacy of Slavery, Racism, and Contemporary Black Activism on Campus." *History of Education Quarterly* 56, no. 4: 646–56.

Buchdahl, Angela. 2024. "A More Forgiving World Is a World Redeemed." Central Synagogue, streamed live on October 12, 2024, YouTube video, 20:29, https://www.youtube.com/watch?v=ThTLNUGFOqg.

CDC NCHHSTP (Centers for Disease Control and Prevention's National Center for HIV, Viral Hepatitis, STD, and Tuberculosis Prevention). 2016. "Half of Black Gay Men and a Quarter of Latino Gay Men Projected to Be Diagnosed Within Their Lifetime." HIV.gov, Feb. 23, 2016. https://www.hiv.gov/blog/half-of-black-gay-men-and-a-quarter-of-latino-gay-men-projected-to-be-diagnosed-within-their-lifetime.

Comstock, Gary David. 1993. *Gay Theology Without Apology.* Cleveland: Pilgrim.

Craig, Shelley L., Ashley Austin, Mitra Rashidi, and Michael Adams. 2017. "Fighting for Survival: The Experiences of Lesbian, Gay, Bisexual, Transgender, and Questioning Students in Religious Colleges and Universities." *Journal of Gay and Lesbian Social Services* 29, no. 1: 1–24.

Croly, George. 1854. *Spirit of God, Descend upon My Heart.* Hymnary.org. Accessed May 11, 2025. https://hymnary.org/text/spirit_of_god_descend_upon_my_heart.

Dias, Elizabeth. 2020. "Christianity Will Have the Power." *New York Times*, August 9, 2020. https://www.nytimes.com/2020/08/09/us/evangelicals-trump-christianity.html.

Dobson, James C. *Bringing Up Boys: Practical Advice and Encouragement for Those Shaping the Next Generation of Men.* Wheaton, IL: Tyndale House Publishers, 2005.

Espey, Richard. 2015. *The Revelation of Bobby Pritchard.* Self-published.

Gardner, Christine J. 2017. "'Created This Way': Liminality, Rhetorical Agency, and the Transformative Power of Constraint Among Gay Christian College Students." *Communication and Critical/Cultural Studies* 14, no. 1: 31–47.

REFERENCES

Gardiner, Judith K. 2011. "Gender and Masculinity Texts: Consensus and Concerns for Feminist Classrooms." In *Masculinity Lessons: Rethinking Men's and Women's Studies*, edited by James V. Catano and Daniel A. Novak, 63–73. Baltimore: Johns Hopkins University Press.

Hamilton, Laura. 2007. "Trading on Heterosexuality: College Women's Gender Strategies and Homophobia." *Gender & Society* 21, no. 2: 145–172.

How, William Walsham. 1864. For All the Saints, Who from Their Labor Rest. Hymnary.org. Accessed May 11, 2025. https://hymnary.org/text/for_all_the_saints_who_from_their_labors.

King, Martin Luther Jr. 1967. *Where Do We Go from Here: Chaos or Community?* New York: Harper & Row.

Koester, Anne Y., ed. 2002. *Liturgy and Justice: To Worship God in Spirit and Truth; Twenty-Ninth Annual Pastoral Liturgy Conference*. Collegeville, MN: Liturgical.

LaHaye, Tim, and Beverly LaHaye. 1998. *The Act of Marriage: The Beauty of Sexual Love*. Grand Rapids, MI: Zondervan.

Lee, Ella. 2022. "Marjorie Taylor Greene, Other Conservatives Lean into Christian Nationalism. What Is It?" *USA Today*, August 9, 2022. https://www.usatoday.com/story/news/politics/2022/08/09/what-is-christian-nationalism/10211671002/.

Lyte, Henry Francis. 1847. Abide with Me. Hymnary.org. Accessed May 11, 2025. https://hymnary.org/text/abide_with_me_fast_falls_the_eventide.

McDowell, Amy D. 2017. "Aggressive and Loving Men: Gender Hegemony in Christian Hardcore Punk." *Gender & Society* 31, no. 2: 223–244.

Milman, Henry Hart. 1827. Ride on! Ride on in Majesty! Hymnary.org. Accessed May 11, 2025. https://hymnary.org/text/ride_on_ride_on_in_majesty.

Mitchell, David T., and Sharon L. Snyder. 2014. *Narrative Prosthesis: Disability and the Dependencies of Discourse*. Ann Arbor: University of Michigan Press.

Mock, Janet. 2014. *Redefining Realness: My Path to Womanhood, Identity, Love, and So Much More*. New York: Atria.

Mollenkott, Virginia R. 2000. "Reading the Bible from Low and Outside: Lesbitransgays as God's Tricksters." In *Take Back the Word: A Queer Reading of the Bible*, edited by Robert E. Goss and Mona West, 13–22. Cleveland: Pilgrim.

Niebuhr, Reinhold. 1929. *Leaves from the Notebook of a Tamed Cynic*. Cleveland: Meridian.

Packard, Josh. 2013. "The Impact of Racial Diversity in the Classroom: Activating the Sociological Imagination." *Teaching Sociology* 41, no. 2: 144–158.

Pascoe, C. J. 2003. "Multiple Masculinities? Teenage Boys Talk About Jocks and Gender." *American Behavioral Scientist* 46, no. 10: 1423–1438.

Perry, Samuel L., and Andrew L. Whitehead. 2021."Linking Evangelical Subculture and Phallically Insecure Masculinity Using Google Searches for Male Enhancement." *Journal for the Scientific Study of Religion* 60, no. 2: 442–453.

REFERENCES

Rinkart, Martin. [1636] 1858. *Now Thank We All Our God*. Translated by Catherine Winkworth. Hymnary.org. Accessed May 11, 2025. https://hymnary.org/text/now_thank_we_all_our_god.

Rohac, Dalibor. 2019. *In Defense of Globalism*. Lanham, MD: Rowman & Littlefield.

Sheldon, Myrna P. 2017. "Wild at Heart: How Sociobiology and Evolutionary Psychology Helped Influence the Construction of Heterosexual Masculinity in American Evangelicalism." *Signs: Journal of Women in Culture & Society* 42, no. 4: 977–998.

Stokes, Emily, and Rebecca Schewe. 2016. "Framing from the Pulpit: A Content Analysis of American Conservative Evangelical Protestant Sermon Rhetoric Discussing LGBT Couples and Marriage." *The Journal of Communication and Religion* 39, no. 3: 59–75.

Solevåg, Anna Rebecca. 2016. "No Nuts? No Problem!: Disability, Stigma, and the Baptized Eunuch in Acts 8:26–40." *Biblical Interpretation* 24, no. 1: 81–99.

Toensing, Holly Joan. 2005. "Women of Sodom and Gomorrah: Collateral Damage in the War Against Homosexuality?" *Journal of Feminist Studies in Religion* 21, no. 2: 61–74.

von Schlegel, Katharina. [1752] 1855. *Be Still, My Soul*. Translated by Jane Borthwick. Hymnary.org. Accessed May 11, 2025. https://hymnary.org/text/be_still_my_soul_the_lord_is_on_thy_side.

Wantland, Ross. 2005. "Feminist Frat Boys?: Fraternity Men in the (Women's Studies) House." *NWSA Journal* 17, no. 2: 156–163.

Weissel, Georg. [1642] 1855. *Lift Up Your Heads, Ye Mighty Gates*. Translated by Catherine Winkworth. Hymnary.org. Accessed May 11, 2025. https://hymnary.org/text/lift_up_your_heads_ye_mighty_gates_behol.

Wesley, Charles. 1739. *Hail the Day That Sees Him Rise*. HymnTime.com. Accessed May 11, 2025. http://www.hymntime.com/tch/htm/h/d/a/y/hdaytshr.htm.

West, Darrell M. 2019. *Divided Politics, Divided Nation: Hyperconflict in the Trump Era*. Washington, D.C.: Brookings Institution.

Whitehead, Andrew L. 2014. "Male and Female He Created Them: Gender Traditionalism, Masculine Images of God, and Attitudes Toward Same-Sex Unions." *Journal for the Scientific Study of Religion* 53, no. 3: 479–496.

Williams, David R., and Lisa A. Cooper. "COVID-19 and Health Equity—A New Kind of 'Herd Immunity.'" *Journal of the American Medical Association* 323, no. 24 (2020) 2478–2480.

Yasim, Sameer. 2020. "Gandhi's Killer Evokes Admiration as Never Before." *New York Times*, February 4, 2020. https://www.nytimes.com/2020/02/04/world/asia/india-gandhi-nathuram-godse.html.

www.ingramcontent.com/pod-product-compliance
Lightning Source LLC
LaVergne TN
LVHW051708080426
835511LV00017B/2803

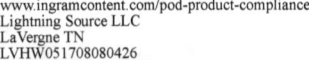